Great things take time;

wait and see.

Still water shows what fish might be.

Breathe, watch, listen;

let hurry pass—

Patience makes small skills last.

Look far ahead;

lift your eyes to sky.

Learn the wind before you fly.

Brave is prepared, not only bold—

Wisdom is warmth in the cold.

Think with care;

choose truth before speed.

A clever plan is the help you need.

Admit mistakes;

that’ s how you grow—

Honest roots help courage show.

Run hard, then rest;

keep a steady pace.

Games teach timing and give joy space.

Practice together;

learn the team’ s song—

Discipline helps fun last long.

Strong alone, stronger together we' ll be.

Share the work and share the sea.

Listen, signal,

help your crew—

Teamwork turns many into true.